ENIGMAS *of* HISTORY

THE SECRETS OF
ANCIENT TOMBS

WORLD
BOOK

a Scott Fetzer company
Chicago
www.worldbook.com

World Book edition of "Enigmas de la historia" by Editorial Sol 90.

Enigmas de la historia
Tumbas antiguas

This edition licensed from Editorial Sol 90 S.L.
Copyright 2013 Editorial Sol S.L. All rights reserved.

English-language revised edition copyright 2014
World Book, Inc.
Enigmas of History
The Secrets of Ancient Tombs

World Book, Inc.
233 North Michigan Avenue
Suite 2000
Chicago, Illinois, 60601 U.S.A.

For information about other World Book publications,
visit our website at **www.worldbook.com** or call
1-800-967-5325.

Library of Congress Cataloging-in-Publication Data

Tumbas antiguas. English.
  The secrets of ancient tombs.
     p. cm. -- (Enigmas of history)
   Summary: "An exploration of the questions and mysteries
that have puzzled scholars and experts about tombs and
burials from ancient times. Features include a map, fact
boxes, biographies of famous experts on burial and tombs,
places to see and visit, a glossary, further readings,
and index"-- Provided by publisher.
  Includes index.
  ISBN 978-0-7166-2661-9
  1. Tombs--Juvenile literature. 2. Excavations (Archaeology)--Juvenile literature. 3. Civilization, Ancient--Juvenile
literature. I. World Book, Inc. II. Title.
CC77.B8S43 2014
930.1--dc23
                                          2014007068

Set ISBN: 978-0-7166-2660-2

Printed in China by PrintWORKS Global Services,
Shenzhen, Guangdong
1st printing May 2014

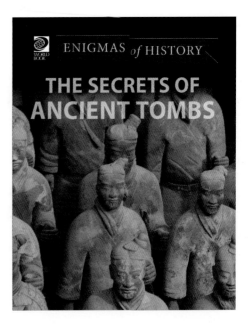

Terra-cotta soldiers were from the tomb complex
of Shi Huangdi, who founded the Qin dynasty in
about 221 B.C. and was China's first emperor.
At Qin's tomb, there are large pits with more than
7,500 life-size, terra-cotta statues of warriors.
Most scholars believe the statues were intended to
guard the emperor in the afterlife.

© RIA Novosti/Alamy Images

Staff

Executive Committee

President
Donald D. Keller

Vice President and Editor in Chief
Paul A. Kobasa

Vice President, Sales
Sean Lockwood

Vice President, Finance
Anthony Doyle

Director, Marketing
Nicholas A. Fryer

Director, Human Resources
Bev Ecker

Editorial

*Associate Director,
Annuals and Topical Reference*
Scott Thomas

*Managing Editor,
Annuals and Topical Reference*
Barbara A. Mayes

*Senior Editor,
Annuals and Topical Reference*
Christine Sullivan

Manager, Indexing Services
David Pofelski

Administrative Assistant
Ethel Matthews

*Manager, Contracts & Compliance
(Rights & Permissions)*
Loranne K. Shields

*Editorial Administration
Director, Systems and Projects*
Tony Tills

*Senior Manager, Publishing
Operations*
Timothy Falk

Manufacturing/Production

Director
Carma Fazio

Manufacturing Manager
Barbara Podczerwinski

*Production/Technology
Manager*
Anne Fritzinger

Proofreader
Nathalie Strassheim

Graphics and Design

Art Director
Tom Evans

Senior Designer
Don Di Sante

Media Researcher
Jeff Heimsath

*Manager, Cartographic
Services*
Wayne K. Pichler

Senior Cartographer
John M. Rejba

Marketing

Marketing Manager
Tamika Robinson

Marketing Specialist
Annie Suhy

Contents

6 The Dead Tell Their Story

8 The Final Resting Place

10 Unveiling the Secrets of Death

16 Who Was Otzi the Iceman?

18 What Happened to the Bog Bodies?

20 Why Did the Egyptians Build the Pyramids?

24 What Is the Tomb of Qin Hiding?

32 The Mysterious Xiaohe Mummies

34 What Mysteries Surround
the Lord of Sipán?

42 Places to See and Visit

44 Glossary

45 For Further Information

46 Index

48 Acknowledgments

The Dead Tell Their Story

All cultures around the world have developed ways of dealing with one of the most significant events in life: its end. Death is something no one has been able to avoid and, therefore, is something we all have in common. The ritual treatment of the dead is considered one of the earliest and most fundamental indicators of culture. But only in the last few decades has technology advanced to where it allows the dead to reveal to us so much about their personal stories and, in a sense, to come back to life. Such technological methods as facial reconstruction, virtual autopsies, 3D modeling, and DNA and isotopic analysis have been applied with stunning results.

(An isotope is one of two or more atoms of the same chemical element that differ in the amount of matter they contain; isotope analysis is the identification of the distribution of certain stable isotopes and chemical elements within chemical compounds.) Through these means, we are now able to find out a good deal about the lives of specific individuals who died without leaving written clues. This knowledge includes information as significant and diverse as the cause of death, the places where they lived, changes in their diet, what diseases they suffered, how they looked when alive, and their perception of an afterlife.

Much of this information comes from studying bodies that have been preserved either through natural or artificial processes. While the vast majority of human remains have not been preserved but are, rather, skeletons, these also provide a large amount of data. That information increases when considering the offerings and other objects found near them.

Human remains have long stimulated human imagination. Mummies are a television documentary staple and never cease to inspire fictional sensation in books and movies and attract crowds to exhibitions. Their educational potential is immense—a means of teaching archaeology, environmental conservation, geography, health, human biology, and nutrition.

This book presents examples of burials from around the world, dating back several millennia—including mummies that predate those of the Egyptians by more than 2,000 years. It focuses on some of the most famous funerary mysteries of the past: Ötzi the Iceman, found in the Italian Alps; the bog bodies of northern Europe; the pyramids of Egypt; the Chinese mausoleum of Qin Shi Huangdi with its terracotta warriors; the Indo-European mummies in the Tarim basin in western China; and the Lord of Sipán in northern Peru.

Since low temperatures are one of the best ways to preserve organic matter, frozen tombs provide access to the past in a way that is unattainable by other means. The information obtained from the research on the Alpine Iceman has revolutionized our understanding of *Neolithic* man. (Neolithic refers to the later Stone Age, marked by the beginning of agriculture and animal husbandry, and the use of polished stone weapons and tools.) Since technology is constantly evolving, the frozen bodies will continue to contribute to human understanding.

The documentation of human remains as well as the discoveries that are made concerning them, have helped deepen our understanding of cultures from around the world. This has contributed to the preservation of a priceless heritage for future generations. Tombs will continue to be discovered, and the documented cases of ancient tombs will never cease to fascinate those who share in humanity's search for meaning in the universe.

The Final Resting Place

Since prehistory, the living have provided their dead with specific places and forms of final rest.
These have taken many forms, from anonymous graves to the Great Pyramid of Giza.

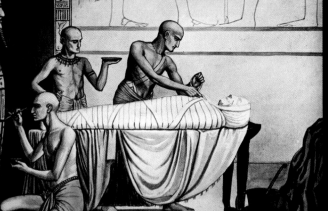

Funerary Practices

Burial is perhaps the most ancient and universal funerary practice, but cremation, ritual devouring by beasts, and releasing the body to the sea have also been widely practiced. Embalming was practiced in ancient Egypt (left) to preserve the body. Natural mummification also occurs in such dry environments as deserts and high mountains.

ETRUSCAN TOMBS in Cerveteri, Italy, with Etruscan funerary gravestones from the 400's–300's B.C.

Unveiling the Secrets of Death

Ancient tombs still hold many mysteries for archaeologists.

With modern technology, ancient tombs have become open books, if not entire encyclopedias. Archaeologists, along with coroners, biologists, biochemists, and DNA specialists, are drawing the family tree of the human species from its earliest origins thanks to increasingly precise techniques and methods for preserving and dating their findings from tombs. What appears in most excavations are objects, for example, pottery shards. But when intact remains of the deceased are found, the picture changes, and even more so if the remains are mummified.

Mummification, when it is not a result of natural causes—dehydration, freezing, or absence of oxygen, as in peat bogs—is a clear indicator of the existence of a complex and well-structured society able to develop tech-

niques for preserving the human body. Mummies allow us to be face to face with a human being who died thousands of years ago. They also open an authentic window into the past.

ANALYSIS OF MUMMIES

Science today not only allows us to study and analyze in depth the bones, skin, and DNA of a human body, but also to reconstruct it. This allows us to know the age and gender of a mummy. We can discern its facial features.

From the study of the guts, skin, and bones, researchers may also know the cause of death: how the individual spent the last days of his or her life; what the individual ate; what diseases the individual may have suffered from; and even how many injuries he or she may have lived through.

However, as we acquire more and more information, the unknowns also increase. This is the case with a very

interesting and outstanding group of more than 100 mummies that were discovered in Chile in 1983. They were found in the Atacama Desert, at Chinchorro, near the Chilean city of Arica.

THE CHINCHORRO PEOPLE

The "Chinchorro people" inhabited the coasts of what are now southern Peru and northern Chile between 9000 and 1500 B.C. Their culture is believed to the oldest in the Americas.

It is known that the Chinchorro people were fishermen who did not practice agriculture and did not use pottery or the loom. They did not leave monuments or writing. The only objects that archaeologists found were some very basic tools and well-crafted shellfish hooks. However, their spiritual lives, given their unusual mummification techniques, must have been complex.

The mummies of the Chinchorro culture are peculiar in

TOMB OF HEROD (ISRAEL)
Aerial view of Herodium, where, according to the first-century, Romano-Jewish historian Josephus, Herod the Great was buried. According to the Gospel of Matthew, Herod the Great ordered the deaths of all Jewish boys age two and under in Bethlehem in an attempt to kill the Messiah foretold by the wise men of the east.

that they were not designed to remain in graves. Rather, they seem to have been made to be worshiped in rituals, to be placed in public places next to the images of the gods, thereby fulfilling the role of protectors of the community. They are like statues, works of art created with the bodies of ancestors. They wear masks and wigs made from human hair. Organs were removed, and the bodies were dismembered to later be reassembled and recovered by the skin. The "body" had an internal structure of sticks and reeds, held together with a paste made from ashes. One of the mummies is about 7,000 years old, fully 2,000 years older than the most ancient of Egyptian mummies. It is believed that the Chinchorro people abandoned the practice of artificial mummification around 1700 B.C. Their successors merely buried their dead in the desert, where many bodies ended up being mummified by extreme dryness.

THE INCA

Among the Inca culture, as well as some pre-Inca South American cultures, mummies were considered *huacas,* powerful beings that provided fertility and good harvests. The huacas connected the natural and the supernatural, humans

to the gods. Of the known Inca mummies, the most famous is the Inca Ice Maiden: a 14-year-old girl who was probably offered as a sacrifice to the gods on a platform built for the occasion at more than 19,685 feet (599 meters) above sea level. She died around 1465, at the time of the Inca ruler Yupanqui.

The Ice Maiden was discovered in 1993 by Johan Reinhard, after the eruption of a volcano thawed the ice that encased her. The extraordinarily well preserved Inca Ice Maiden has provided invaluable information to historians. The

DNA analysis, for example, revealed that her father was a native of a village in what is now Panama.

But Chile and Peru are just two of many places in the world where mummies of great archaeological value have been found.

ANCIENT EGYPT

In ancient Egypt, mummifying was carried out for more than 3,000 years. Initially, only the pharaohs and leading members of the priestly class were mummified; eventually, other significant people were mummified; and toward the end, any citizen who could afford

CHINCHORRO

The mummies of the Chinchorro culture are styled according to age: they are black, red, or have a patina of clay (above left).

NEWGRANGE MAUSOLEUM

(above) is one of the most monumental examples of mound tomb culture, which was common in what is now Europe in the late Stone Age (about 3370 to 2920 B.C.). Inside the tomb is a stone richly decorated with spirals (inset above) that is illuminated by the sun one week before and one week after the winter solstice.

it. Despite the long history of this custom, modern science has never been able to say with certainty what technique the Egyptian embalmers actually used. Mummification was an oral tradition, and its secrets were passed on by the best teachers. No text or painting has ever been found describing or illustrating the procedures that were used. While the Greek historian Herodotus gave some clues, they were merely hearsay.

Today, scientists can only surmise how it was performed. However, in 1994, scientists carried out a mummification

process in a laboratory in the United States (consented to before death by the person experimented upon). The outcome was considered a success.

NEWGRANGE

The oldest tombs continue to hide ancient mysteries. One of these is the prehistoric *necropolis* (cemetery) of *Brú na Bóinne* (palace of the Boyne, in Irish Gaelic) including the Newgrange passage tomb, in the Boyne River Valley. Newgrange is a monument built by a *Neolithic* culture between 3370 and 2920 B.C. (Neolithic refers to the late part of the

Stone Age.) Newgrange was discovered in the 1600's and excavated between 1962 and 1975.

It is a large circular mound covering an area 230 feet (70 meters) in diameter, made with 97 large stones topped by a white quartz and granite wall leaning inward. A 55-foot (32-meter) passage leads to a *cruciform* (cross-shaped) chamber with a roof that has remained intact for more than 6,000 years and where funerary rituals may have been carried out. Large stone vessels have been found there contain-

ing the cremated remains of at least five individuals.

The structure is aligned with the sun and has a narrow opening of about 4 inches (10 centimeters) above the entrance. On the winter solstice in the Northern Hemisphere, the sun's rays enter the opening and—for about 17 minutes—illuminate the passage all the way to the center of the chamber. Some believe that human sacrifices were made in this chamber, but generally it is considered to have been a sacred *columbarium* holding the ashes of important people, who would have been cremated outside. The truth is that besides the age of the site, everything else is conjecture. No one knows for certain which culture erected it, and there are no other known remains of their civilization. All that remains is this unusual *Neolithic* (late Stone Age) monument, made of carved stones engraved with spiral, circle, and zigzag patterns.

THE TERRA-COTTA ARMY

Under another mountain there is a tomb that has not yet revealed its secrets and which still holds the remains of a person who was considered sacred in his time. His tomb was actually surrounded by a replica of his entire empire for his final voyage. This is the tomb of the first emperor and unifier of China, Qin Shi Huangdi, whose body, according to his wish, is believed to lie beneath a mountain of earth planted with trees so that he would not be found. The emperor died in 210 B.C., and his immense grave was ignored until A.D. 1974, when farmers digging a well discovered some of the thousands of terracotta figures that were buried there, representing his great army.

Also worth noting are a group of mummies discovered by Aurel Stein in the Tarim Basin in China in the late 1800's. They date from between 4,000 and 2,000 B.C. and have a peculiarity: They are quite tall in stature for ancient people and have Caucasian features. Why they were in what is now western China remains a mystery.

HUACA RAJADA

In 1987, the tombs at Huaca Rajada were discovered by archaeologist Walter Alva. They are located near the town of Sipán in the middle of the Lambayeque Valley in northern Peru. In Quechua, a Native American language of South America, a huaca is an object or place that represents something revered; rajada

means cracked. The burial site was named *huaca rajada* because it had been "cracked" by grave robbers before Alva "discovered" it.

The tombs contained the remains of the Lord of Sipán as well as a rich array of funerary goods. The discovery led to a rewriting of the history of the *pre-Columbian* (before 1492) Americas and of the Moche people—an American Indian culture that flourished in the coastal desert of what is now northern Peru from the A.D. 100's to the 700's. Moche rulers were considered to be demigods. The royal mausoleum of Sipán was built in the A.D 100's. So far, nearly 70 tombs have been excavated there.

HERODIUM

According to tradition, Herod, king of Judea from 37 to 4 B.C., was buried in Herodium, a fortress-palace that he had built atop a hill in what is now the West Bank, 7 miles (11 kilometers) south of Jerusalem. A tomb was discovered there in 2007 by archaeologist Ehud Netzer of the Hebrew University of Jerusalem. Although no inscription has been found that proves it was the tomb of the king, a sarcophagus broken into hundreds of pieces has been found, which could have been his.

THE ICEMAN

Ötzi the Iceman was discovered in the Italian Alps in 1991. He was about 40 years old when he died some 5,300 years ago. Objects found with him have provided insights into his world.

There is also mystery surrounding another large group of mummies known as the "bog bodies." More than a thousand of them have been found in bogs in northern Europe. Some are 2,000 years old, and almost all of them show signs of violent deaths.

Victor Henry Mair
(1943–)

Professor of Chinese studies at the University of Pennsylvania since 1979, Mair was part of the interdisciplinary team that studied the Caucasian mummies of the Tarim Basin in China. Based on the experience, he wrote *The Tarim Mummies: Ancient China and the Mystery of the Earliest Peoples from the West.* The book analyzes the role Central Asia played in intercultural connections between East and West.

Johan Reinhard
(1943–)

Born in Illinois, American explorer Johan Reinhard completed his Ph.D. in anthropology in Vienna and is an expert in mountain archaeology. He specializes in researching the villages of the Andes and has discovered numerous famous mummies on several Andean peaks.

MOUNTAINEER. Reinhard's discovery of the mummies in Ampato and Llullaillaco, at high altitude, confirmed the ritual sacrifice of young Inca.

Walter Alva (1951–)

This Peruvian archaeologist gained international fame in 1987. After being warned by the police that grave robbers were looting an adobe pyramid in the enclosure of Huaca Rajada, in Sipán, he found the mausoleum of a powerful Moche ruler, who has been given the name "the Lord of Sipán." This discovery was considered to be the most significant of pre-Columbian archaeology finds. Alva, director of the Brünning Archaeological Museum of Lambayeque—his home province—and also the modern Museum of the Royal Tombs of Sipán, is an authority on the Moche culture, which flourished in northern Peru from the A.D. 100's to the 700's. He has been honored by the Peruvian government with the Order of the Sun—the highest award bestowed by Peru to commend notable civil and military merit. His excavations have helped increase awareness of pre-Inca cultures in South America. In 2007, he discovered the murals of the temple of Ventarrón, which date back 4,000 years and are considered the oldest in the Americas.

REVELATION. The discovery of the Lord of Sipán revealed that the pyramids of Huaca Rajada were part of the Moche culture and not the Chimú culture as was previously believed.

Xu Weihong (1966–)

With a degree in archaeology from the University of Gansu, Xu is the director of the archaeological team that unearthed the famous terra-cotta warriors. She has been devoted to their preservation since 1989, the year she joined the Museum of Xi'an. Under the direction of Xu Weihong, new sites linked to the mausoleum of Qin Shi Huangdi have been explored. According to Xu Weihong, archaeological findings seem to confirm the legends about the tomb of the first Chinese emperor. Her work in research and preservation has been internationally recognized.

Ehud Netzer (1934– 2010)

An Israeli architect, professor, and tenacious archaeologist, Netzer specialized in the architecture of Herod's reign. He began excavations at Herodium in 1972. After 25 years of work, he found a broken sarcophagus identical to that described by first-century historian Josephus.

Who Was Ötzi the Iceman?

The Iceman, whom scientists have named Ötzi, is the oldest known mummy from Europe. He was discovered in 1991 in an alpine glacier. His tools, found with the body, have revealed a great deal about life in what is now Europe 5,300 years ago.

On Sept. 19, 1991, a pair of German hikers, Helmut and Erika Simon, discovered a human body protruding from a half-frozen puddle in the alpine valley of Ötzi, between Italy and Austria. They believed they had happened upon the victim of an accident and told the police, who immediately removed the body. Surprisingly, it turned out to be the body of a man who had died some 5,300 years before. He was mummified. A bow made of yew wood was found beside him, as well as two finished arrows and material for making viburnum wood arrows. The finished arrows had guide feathers and flint arrowheads attached to the shaft with birch sap and string. He also carried a birch-bark bag, a fiber rope, a flint knife, a chisel, a bear skin cloak, a little tinder and pyrite for making fire, and a copper hatchet with a lime-wood handle. He had a wound on his hand and another on his back, where an arrowhead had entered and punctured his left lung. How did he die? DNA analysis revealed the blood of other people on the cloak and knife. He probably died of blood loss after a battle with rivals.

BIOLOGICAL ANALYSIS

Ötzi has been studied in depth. He was 5 feet 5 inches (1.65 meters) tall, was not over 45 years old, and weighed about 110 pounds (50 kilograms). The pollen found on his body was analyzed and revealed information regarding wheat and legume crops in his surroundings. The remains of his digestive system led to the conclusion that he had eaten twice not long before his death: a meal of *chamois* meat (small goat-like animal that lives in high mountains) and another of deer meat. He had also consumed cereals, blackthorn shrub, and some roots.

The presence of parallel lines tattooed on his left wrist, lumbar area, and both legs, coinciding with signs of arthritis, led to the conclusion that they had some magic-curative purpose. His clothing was quite sophisticated. He wore a leather vest and cloak. His footwear was water resistant and designed for use in snow, though it could have been the upper part of some kind of snow shoe.

The Iceman was quite an intelligent man—an artisan, hunter, and perhaps also shepherd and farmer, capable of living in mountains 10,500 feet (3,200 meters) above sea level.

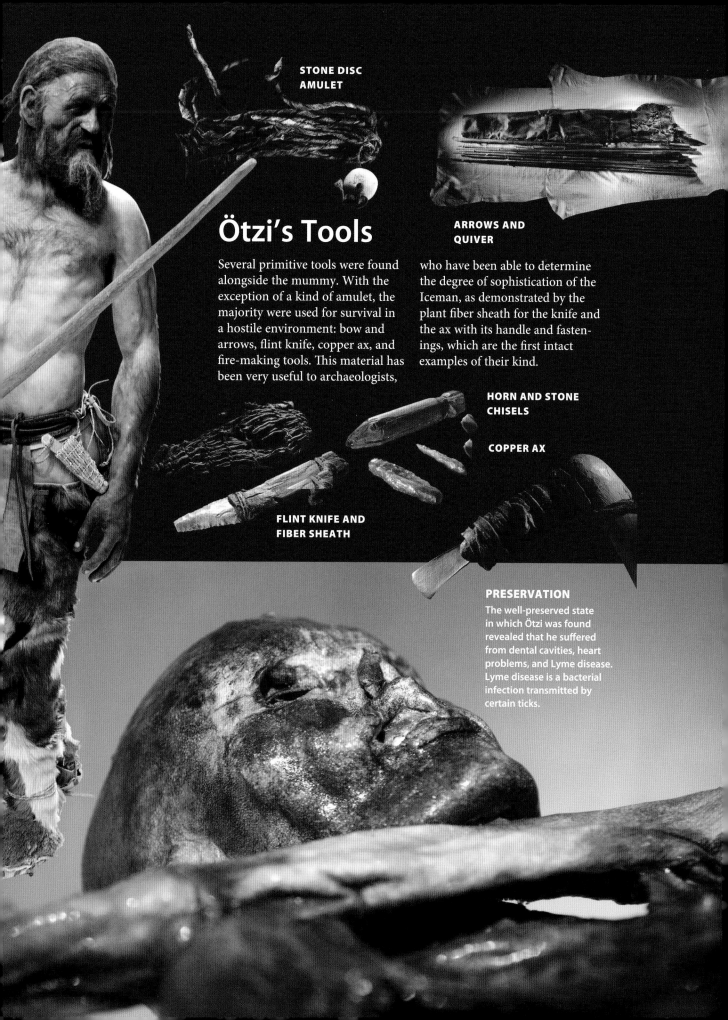

**STONE DISC
AMULET**

Ötzi's Tools

Several primitive tools were found
alongside the mummy. With the
exception of a kind of amulet, the
majority were used for survival in
a hostile environment: bow and
arrows, flint knife, copper ax, and
fire-making tools. This material has
been very useful to archaeologists,

who have been able to determine
the degree of sophistication of the
Iceman, as demonstrated by the
plant fiber sheath for the knife and
the ax with its handle and fasten-
ings, which are the first intact
examples of their kind.

**ARROWS AND
QUIVER**

**HORN AND STONE
CHISELS**

COPPER AX

**FLINT KNIFE AND
FIBER SHEATH**

PRESERVATION

The well-preserved state
in which Ötzi was found
revealed that he suffered
from dental cavities, heart
problems, and Lyme disease.
Lyme disease is a bacterial
infection transmitted by
certain ticks.

What Happened to the Bog Bodies?

Since the 1800's, more than 1,000 mummified bodies have been uncovered in the peat bogs of northern Europe. The majority of them have one distinctive feature in common—they died violently.

They are known as the "bog bodies" because they were uncovered in the peat bogs of northern Europe—Denmark, Germany, Ireland, and the United Kingdom. Peat is partly decayed plant matter that has collected in swamps and marshes over long periods of time. The lack of oxygen in these wetlands inhibits the natural decay of organic material, which is how bodies remained in a mummified state for some 2,500 years. While they were discovered in different places, they have a common characteristic. Almost all show signs of a violent death: strangulation marks or the remains of rope around the neck; signs of having been *bludgeoned* (hit repeatedly with a heavy object); others were decapitated or stabbed; while still others had been thrown into the bog alive and drowned. Almost all were naked and had a birch rod on or driven into their body. Were they sacrificed to the gods? Or were they law breakers or prisoners of war sentenced to death?

RITUAL SACRIFICE

Scientists have generally concluded that the bog bodies were sacrifices. It is known that in northern Europe the bogs were held sacred by the people who lived in the region. They believed that such deities as Nerthus—goddess of the earth honored by the inhabitants of the Jutland peninsula in present-day Denmark—resided there. The bog bodies could have been sacrificed to her.

Other scientists have linked their deaths to fertility rituals. Julius Caesar noted that peat bog sacrifices were common practice after winning a battle in honor of the gods of war. On the other hand, the Roman historians Pliny the Elder and Tacitus recorded that these people had the custom of drowning criminals, deserters, traitors, and adulterers in bogs.

Analysis of the contents of the victims' stomachs seems to confirm the ritual sacrifice theory. Scientific analysis has revealed that they consumed certain plant materials that were used in various religious ceremonies at the time. The bog body known as the "Lindow Man," discovered near Manchester, England, in 1984, was found to have had mistletoe fruit in his stomach. This led scientists to theorize that he was the victim of a ritual. In the stomach of the Grauballe Man, found in present-day Denmark in 1952, were remains of rye ergot, which indicates that he may have been drugged.

The Tollund Man

The Tollund Man was discovered in a bog in Denmark in 1950. This Scandinavian tribe member from the 300's B.C. was 5 feet 2 inches (1.57 meters) tall and was 30 to 40 years old when he died. He was found dressed

around his neck, with which he had been strangled. The one difference between the Tollund Man and other bog bodies is that Tollund Man has a calm expression on his face, suggesting that he accepted his fate as a

Why Did the Egyptians Build the Pyramids?

Tombs for pharaohs and the wealthy in ancient Egypt were much more elaborate than burials for the poor. Egypt's pyramids are among the largest and most famous tombs in the world. The pyramids—gigantic structures made of stone blocks—are marvels of ancient architecture.

The ruins of 35 major pyramids still stand near the Nile River in Egypt. Each was built to protect the body of an Egyptian king buried inside or beneath the pyramid in a secret chamber that was filled with treasures of gold and precious objects. The three largest Egyptian pyramids are found at Giza. The tomb of the pharaoh Khufu (also known as Cheops), called the *Great Pyramid,* is the largest. It was built from more than 2 million stone blocks that average 2 1/2 tons (2.3 metric tons) each. The Great Pyramid today stands about 450 feet (140 meters) high.

Khufu's burial chamber is inside the Great Pyramid. A corridor leads from an entrance to several rooms within the pyramid. One of the rooms is called the *Queen's Chamber,* though the queen is not buried there. Khufu had a burial chamber built for himself, called the *King's Chamber.* A long corridor called the *Grand Gallery* leads to Khufu's chamber.

Ancient Egyptians who built the pyramids had no machinery or iron tools. To construct the monuments, they cut huge limestone blocks with copper chisels and saws. Most of the stone came from nearby limestone deposits. Historians believe gangs of men dragged the blocks to the pyramid site and pushed the first layer of stones into place. Then they built long ramps of earth and brick, and dragged the stones up the ramps to form the next layer. As they finished each layer, they raised and lengthened the ramps. Finally, they covered the pyramid with an outer coating of white casing stones. They laid these outer stones so exactly that from a distance the pyramid appeared to have been from a single white stone.

The Pyramids, however, could not protect the pharaohs of ancient Egypt. Long ago, thieves broke into the pyramids and stole the treasures they contained. Later pharaohs stopped building pyramids. Tutankhamun, like other pharaohs of his era, built secret tombs hidden in cliffs that are found near modern-day Cairo, the capital of Egypt. Some kings of the Kushite kingdom in Nubia, south of Egypt, built pyramids long after they were no longer used in Egypt.

Egyptian Mummies

The ancient Egyptians mummified their dead because they believed the body had to be preserved for use in the afterlife. The most famous mummies are probably those of Ramses II and Tutankhamun, who were *pharaohs* (rulers) of ancient Egypt.

By about 2600 B.C., the Egyptians had developed an elaborate process of preparing mummies. The Ancient Egyptians believed that when a person died, his or her spirit was released from the body. In order to have a good afterlife, the spirit needed to come back to its body. They developed mummification as a way to preserve a dead body so it was recognizable and usable for the spirit after death.

Although ancient texts related certain details of Egyptian mummification, the exact process remains a mystery. It is known that skilled workers removed the stomach, liver, lungs, and intestines from the body through a small incision made on the left side of the abdomen. The heart, which the Egyptians considered the center of reasoning, was usually left in place. In some cases, workers removed the brain with a hook through a hole pierced through the nose.

The body and organs were then covered with *natron,* a powdery mixture of salt and sodium carbonate or sodium bicarbonate. Natron acted to draw moisture out of the body tissues. After the body was dried, it was treated with certain perfumes and resins that helped seal out moisture. The body could be stuffed with straw, linen, moss,

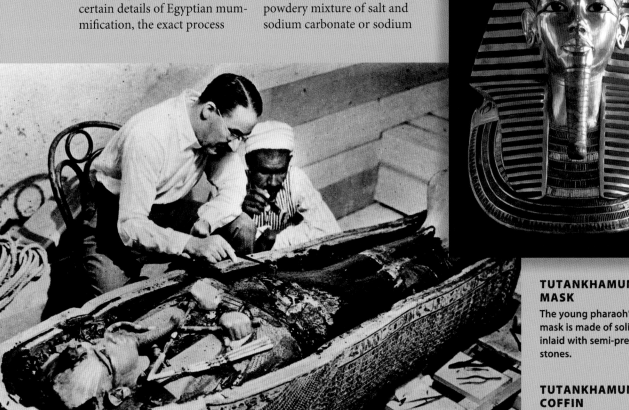

TUTANKHAMUN'S MASK

The young pharaoh's death mask is made of solid gold inlaid with semi-precious stones.

TUTANKHAMUN'S COFFIN

British archaeologist Howard Carter and an Egyptian assistant clean Tutankhamun's coffin after its discovery in 1922.

EGYPTIAN MUMMIES

Egyptian mummies were wound tightly with linen and then laid out in coffins. In some periods of Egyptian history, the coffins were painted (far right).

CANOPIC JAR

The internal organs extracted from a body before mummification were usually placed in the tomb in separate containers called canopic jars.

or other material to give it a more lifelike appearance.

Once the body was sufficiently dried, it was then thoroughly wrapped in linen bandages. The wrapped body, now a mummy, was placed in a coffin or a series of coffins, one inside the other. The coffins were made of wood or stone and were sometimes shaped like the body and decorated. The internal organs were usually placed in the tomb in separate containers called *canopic jars*. Mummies in their coffins were often buried in underground tombs.

Archaeologists excavating in the huge burial ground called the Valley of the Kings, near Luxor in Egypt, have uncovered hundreds of mummies. They have even been able to learn the identity of some

of the mummies. For example, archaeologists have identified the mummy of Ramses II, one of the most celebrated kings of ancient Egypt. He reigned from about 1279 to 1213 B.C.

In 1922, British archaeologist Howard Carter discovered the tomb and mummy of the pharaoh Tutankhamun, popularly known as "King Tut." Historians believe Tutankhamun died sometime around 1322 B.C. at about the age of 18.

Carter discovered that his tomb had not been opened since ancient times. The coffin still contained Tutankhamun's mummy, and the tomb held hundreds of magnificent treasures that had been buried with him. It is the only tomb of an Egyptian pharaoh to be discovered almost completely undamaged.

What Is the Tomb of Qin Hiding?

The tomb of the first emperor of China, Qin Shi Huangdi, holds one of history's most fascinating funerary mysteries. The tomb is one of the most important archaeological sites ever discovered. Yet, the vast majority of it has not been excavated.

In 1974, a group of farmers began digging a well near Mount Li, around 19 miles (30 kilometers) east of the Chinese city of Xi'an, capital and largest city of the Shaanxi Province. At a depth of 20 feet (6 meters), they uncovered colored pieces of what appeared to be clay, life-size statues of soldiers. They had found the first remains of a large terra-cotta army that had been hidden for 2,000 years, guarding the eternal dream of Qin (*chihn*) Shi Huangdi.

The farmers had hit on the lost mausoleum of the unifier and first emperor of China. (The name China is derived from Qin.) According to ancient chronicles, in addition to the first sec-tions of the Great Wall of China, this ruler built a tomb full of marvels—a funeral enclosure of such magnitude that it took 38 years to create. Declared a UNESCO World Heritage Site in 1987, the main parts of the mausoleum remain unexplored.

THE XI'AN WARRIORS

The army of terra-cotta sol-diers was found 1 mile (1.6 kilometers) from the foot of Mount Li, where the emperor's tomb is located. The army consists of 8,000 statues around 5 feet 10 inches (1.77 meters) tall, each with a *unique* (one of a kind) head and face. Their uniforms and shields are exquisitely detailed and correspond to their military rank. The weapons found with the statues are made of bronze. Others are plated with chrome. The army includes foot sol-diers in combat formation; archers and crossbow-men; cavalry riders; and horse-drawn chariots with coachmen and soldiers. The statues are solid from the waist down and hollow from the waist up.

Four pits have been uncovered at the site since 1974. The first held a com-plete foot soldier regiment; the second, 1,400 statues of warriors and horses and 64 chariots; the third appears to be a representa-tion of a general garrison, with 68 high-ranking officials, and the supreme commander's carriage, though his statue is miss-ing. The fourth was empty, which led many archaeolo-gists to conclude that the burial complex had never been completed.

Why Do the Warriors' Faces Vary?

The Xi`an warriors were not the first to stand guard over a royal tomb. Archaeologists have uncovered statues that served the same purpose in *mausoleums* (a large tomb, especially one above ground) from earlier regional rulers. However, apart from the number of troops, Qin's terra-cotta army has two unique qualities: the height of the statues and their distinctive faces. Other funerary armies, before or afterward, were always made up of statues with impersonal faces.

Why this variation in the faces? Perhaps the answer is that Qin hoped to expand his immense power beyond his death and, as a demonstration of his enormous ability, wanted to have as faithful an image as possible of the loyal troops that had exalted him in life.

UNARMED
The terra-cotta soldiers originally carried real bronze weapons. Scientists speculate that they were stripped of their weapons during the civil war that erupted soon after Shi Huangdi's death.

Horses and Tombs

The emperor's Carriage of Tranquility (right) was cast in bronze. The horses are terra cotta.

According to ancient Chinese tradition, death is the continuation of earthly life in the afterlife. For that reason, Shi Huangdi's tomb contained furniture, objects, and riches that were intended not only to make his eternal life more pleasant, but also demonstrate his social status. The sacrifice of horses may have been a funerary demonstration of authority that predated Shi Hungdi. In his tomb, this demonstration was taken to a superlative level, reflecting his absolute supremacy: The horses were buried alive, imitating the royal cavalries. Terra-cotta replicas were made; the carriages were copied in bronze.

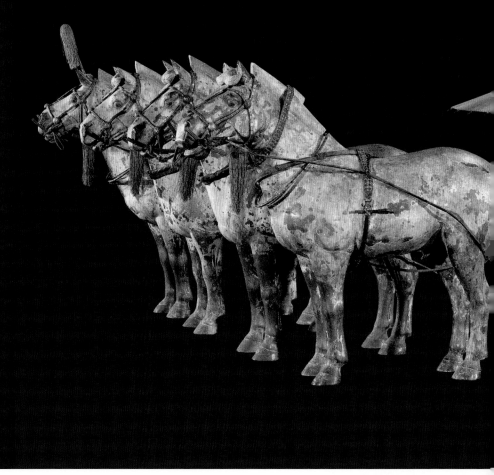

The warriors were perfectly aligned in formation. The floors of the pits were tiled and the pits' sides, corners, and ceilings were reinforced with wooden beams and mats of woven fibers plastered over.

All the statues were painted in bright colors, though their brilliance quickly faded when exposed to oxygen. As a result, excavations in recent years have been carried out with extreme care to avoid losing valuable information.

THE TOMB
Shi Huangdi's tomb is pyramidal in form and is 164 feet (50 meters) high. Its location and form were chosen based on very specific guidelines dictated by an ancient geomantic tradition. The tomb was constructed outside Shi Huangdi's new capital, Xianyang, where he had made local chieftans relocate. (Xianyang is near present-day city of Xi'an.)

The burial mound complex is protected by exterior and interior walls. They enclose an area of 518 acres (209 hectares). Various funerary buildings have been discovered to the north of this wall, which probably formed part of a wing of the Dream Palace (an allusion to death), in which a number of the emperor's *concubines* (a wife who has an inferior rank or rights) may have been buried. There are no immediate plans to excavate the tomb.

CHRONICLES OF SIMA QIAN
All that is known about the mausoleum has come down from Sima Qian, a historian who lived during the Han dynasty (sometime after the fall of the Qin dynasty in 206 B.C.). His book *Shi Ji* (Historical Memories) describes that during the tomb's construction, "three underground channels were dug out for dumping copper melted in the area outside the tomb, while the burial chamber was filled with model palaces, towers, and public buildings, as well as valuable utensils, precious stones and curious objects."

Thanks to the translations of Sima Qian's work, we know that by the emperor's authority, "on the outside of the chamber, the artisans placed automatic crossbows capable of killing any tomb raiders caught in the act" and that inside "they made artificial rivers of mercury flow mechanically, imitating the Yellow and Yangtze rivers and the ocean." "On the upper part," the historian wrote, "they painted the firmament with all of the constellations, while

Slaves and Debts

According to historical records, the 700,000 people that worked in Qin Shi Huangdi's mausoleum were part of three different groups. The first group consisted of technicians and artisans who managed the operation; the second were prisoners of war and enslaved individuals from all over the empire; and the third group was made up of criminals and those convicted as debtors. During this period, whoever broke the law had to pay a fine. If they could not pay it, they were sent to work. Many died because of the arduous work. The expert artisans ended up being buried alive, condemned to keep the secrets of the tomb forever.

Shi Huangdi

Considered the founder of the centralized and totalitarian Chinese Empire that lasted for millennia, Qin Shi Huangdi (259?-210 B.C.) was a ruler of legendary accomplishment, akin to Alexander the Great or Julius Caesar in the West. He unified the country, the language, the currency, the units of measurement, and the length of the shafts of Chinese carriages. He created a bureaucratic system based on merit and began work on the Great Wall of China. An audacious and cruel strategist, he conquered rival kingdoms in merely a decade. One of his great obsessions was the quest for immortality.

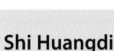

the Earth was represented on the lower part." Other translators describe the ceiling of the room as, "bronze, sprinkled with gems, as if it was a star-strewn sky."

The great mausoleum of Qin Shi Huangdi still retains its mystery, as well as the corpses of all those whom destiny made "assistants of the eternal dream" of the emperor who made China one single kingdom. We do not know how many "assistants" there were, but we have a good idea of how they died. Sima Qian wrote: "Immediately after the emperor was placed in the burial chamber, surrounded by his treasures, the interior

and exterior doors were closed, imprisoning all those who had worked in his mausoleum. Nobody could get out." According to Sima Qian, the concubines who had not borne the emperor's children were also buried alive in the mausoleum.

Emperer Qin Shi Huangdi died in 210 B.C. His son proved to be a weak ruler, and rebellions began in 209 B.C. The Qin dynasty soon collapsed, and the Han gained control of China.

The tomb's dark secrets will be unveiled when technology permits extensive exploration without harming the contents.

Archaeological Excavation

Excavating a tomb is an enormous undertaking, requiring coordination between numerous professionals. This is all the more true when the site is as colossal as the one at Xi`an, which presents technical difficulties as well. For these reasons, the majority of this burial enclosure has yet to be excavated.

Where to Start

Before commencing an excavation, preliminary data must be gathered concerning the site by surveying the surface and performing archaeological tests. Other preparations must also be carried out: requesting permits, formulating a proposal, and evaluating what tools are needed. The most appropriate method and procedures for the excavation are then decided upon.

1 PREPARING THE GROUND

Before excavation, it is best to clear the surface of the ground to eliminate vegetation and any debris present. Then a sounding is taken to study the strata of the terrain and divide up the terrain according to the selected work method. Measuring lines are placed to mark the exact location of the artifacts.

YELLOW EARTH

To mold the figures, "yellow earth" was used, which is present in the area surrounding the mausoleum.

2 EXCAVATE AND RECORD ACTIONS TAKEN

The terrain is now ready to be excavated. Earth is extracted until the first artifacts are found. It is essential to keep exhaustive records of the actions taken, making thorough notes on the data collected for each discovery.

3 CLEANING THE ARTIFACTS

As walls, pieces of art, or any other type of artifact are found, they are carefully cleaned using different kinds of brushes. If necessary, the objects are sprayed with water so the dirt gives way more easily. Cleaning is sometimes done outside the site.

The Xi'an Dilemma

Unfortunately, much of the vivid original colors of the terra-cotta warriors was lost due to oxidation. This happened within hours after they were unearthed. As a result, some archaeologists believe that more advanced technology is needed before proceeding with the excavation of Qin's tomb.

THOUSANDS OF PIECES
The nearly 8,000 warriors were made in pieces. The torso and appendages were made with molds, while the faces were personalized—no two are alike. Reconstructing the figures was a real puzzle for the archaeologists.

7 REPRODUCING THE PROCESS
To understand exactly how the Xi`an figures were created, archaeologists recreated the entire process. The shaping, baking, and finishing of the warriors were tested using various methods until they matched the technique employed by the original artisans.

6 RESTORATION AND CONCLUSIONS
Along with the restoration of damaged artifacts—in Xi`an, many figures had to be reconstructed—the team of archaeologists begins analyzing the results of the excavation. Conclusions are published afterwards in the form of a memorandum, report, or article.

4 PROTECTING THE ARTIFACTS
In many cases, the discovered artifacts demand special protection to keep them from deteriorating upon contact with oxygen. In the case of the terra-cotta warriors, it was necessary to spray the figures with chemicals to prevent deterioration.

5 CLASSIFICATION
Once the work of excavating the tomb is complete, the artifacts are classified. A serial number is given to each artifact—a procedure known as cataloging—and an informational inventory is created.

The Eighth Wonder

Emperor Qin Shi Huangdi (259?-210 B.C.), the first ruler to unify China, left behind a tomb as grand as his legacy. While it was ignored for centuries, an accidental discovery in 1974 gave archaeologists the clue to finding one of the most spectacular treasures of humanity, considered by some the "eighth wonder of the world."

The Grand Mausoleum of the Emperor

The desire for immortality had always plagued Qin Shi Huangdi. Shortly after making himself emporer, he began building his monumental tomb. With each of his military conquests, the number of workers at the site increased until there were 700,000 working toward completing his funerary obsession. After his death, the work was discontinued.

Hidden Pyramid
It is believed that under the earthen mound of the mausoleum there is a hidden pyramid where the emperor's sarcophagus rests. Since the tomb has not been excavated, this rendering is based on the descriptions of Sima Quin, the second century B.C. historian.

Bronze Chariots
Two full-scale replicas of bronze chariots were found.

Exterior Wall

345 m

350 m

Site of Civil Servants

Sarcophagus Chamber
According to Sima Quian, the emperor's bronze coffin was laid to rest in a room also made of bronze. The ceiling was painted blue. The floor featured a map showing the unification of China.

Site of Acrobats

CHRONOLOGY OF FINDINGS

1974	1976	1980	1998	1999	2000
The first pit with terra-cotta warriors was discovered.	Skeletons of horses buried alive in imperial stables were found.	Two full-scale bronze chariots found.	Ceremonial armor and helmet found, decorated with stone tiles.	Site of full-scale terra-cotta people discovered.	Site found with 12 terra-cotta civil servants and horse skeletons; another with 46 different bronze birds.

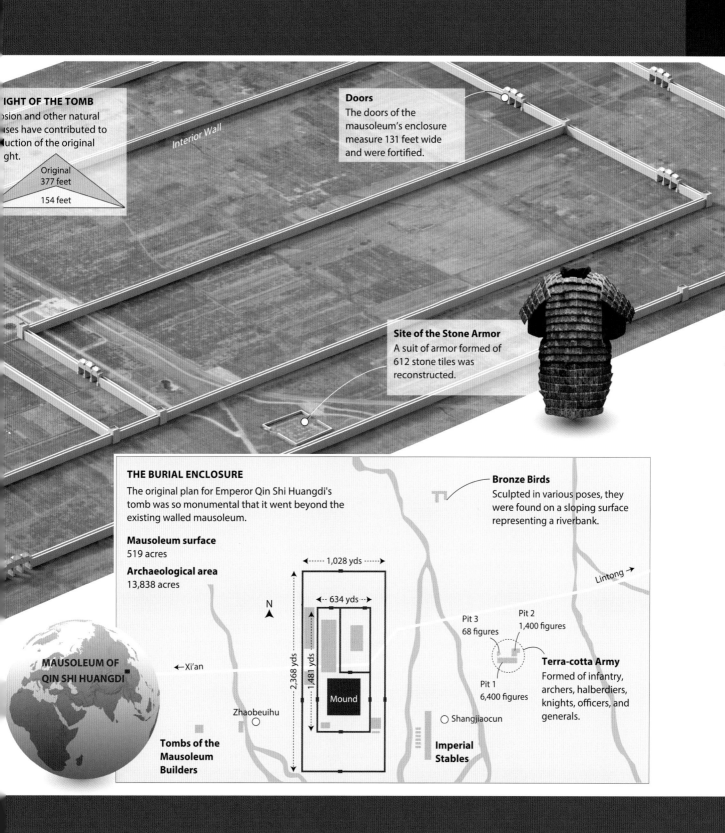

IGHT OF THE TOMB
[ero]sion and other natural
[cau]ses have contributed to
[red]uction of the original
[hei]ght.

Original
377 feet

154 feet

Doors
The doors of the
mausoleum's enclosure
measure 131 feet wide
and were fortified.

Interior Wall

Site of the Stone Armor
A suit of armor formed of
612 stone tiles was
reconstructed.

THE BURIAL ENCLOSURE
The original plan for Emperor Qin Shi Huangdi's
tomb was so monumental that it went beyond the
existing walled mausoleum.

Mausoleum surface
519 acres

Archaeological area
13,838 acres

Bronze Birds
Sculpted in various poses, they
were found on a sloping surface
representing a riverbank.

Lintong →

1,028 yds

634 yds

N

2,368 yds

1,481 yds

Mound

Pit 3
68 figures

Pit 2
1,400 figures

Pit 1
6,400 figures

Terra-cotta Army
Formed of infantry,
archers, halberdiers,
knights, officers, and
generals.

**MAUSOLEUM OF
QIN SHI HUANGDI**

← Xi'an

Zhaobeuihu

○ Shangjiaocun

**Tombs of the
Mausoleum
Builders**

**Imperial
Stables**

The Mysterious Xiaohe Mummies

Some 4,000 years ago, a group of men, women, and children were buried in a desert in central Asia. Their mummies, found in 1934, hinted at European origins. What were they doing in central Asia?

In 1934, in the so-called Xiaohe Little River Tomb complex, Swedish archaeologist Folke Bergman discovered a group of highly unusual mummies in what is now the Xinjiang Uyghur Autonomous Region of western China. Bergman excavated 12 graves and removed approximately 200 artifacts, which he took back to Stockholm. Bergman noted the surprising resemblance in the clothing to Bronze Age grave finds in Denmark, but dismissed any direct connection. (The Bronze Age was the period when people began to use bronze, an alloy of copper and tin, for tools and weapons—about 3500 B.C.) The sands of the salt desert of Taklamakan had preserved the bodies nearly intact. The oldest was some 4,000 years old.

Not much attention was paid to Bergman's finds for almost 70 years. In 2003, scientists began to study the features of the Xiaohe mummies and decided they could be Indo-European in origin. They had light-colored eyes, straight noses, brown hair, and were of large stature. (Some women were over 6 feet [1.8 meters] tall.)

However, genetic analysis revealed that they were Eurasian, a mix from West and East. Under what circumstances Indo-Europeans migrated deep into Asia and interbred with local peoples remains a mystery.

FUNERARY COMPLEX

An excavation project begun in 2003 at Xiaohe revealed more than 160 major tombs and hundreds of smaller tombs. The mummies were buried in coffins shaped like an upside-down boat hull covered with ox hides.

The bodies were dressed in very sophisticated fabrics. Some were woven with designs similar to the tartans plaids worn by Scottish clans. They wore large woolen capes with tassels and leather boots. Many of the mummies wore pointed caps or felt hats with jaunty feathers.

Some faces were covered by masks of wood and metal. Others had two blue stones covering their eyes.

The gravesites were marked with posts 13 feet (10 meters) high. Graves of males have oar-shaped posts. Several items in the burials resemble artifacts familiar in Europe, including offerings in beautifully decorated baskets.

The Xiaohe mummies confounded archaeologists, forcing them to question accepted theories about relationships between human communities before recorded history.

THE BEAUTY OF XIAOHE

A 3,800-year-old mummy, the Beauty of Xiaohe, is among the hundreds of mummies with Indo-European features found at the Small River Cemetery in the Chinese province of Xinjiang.

What Mysteries Surround the Lord of Sipán?

In one of the great archaeological finds of all time, a tomb and a mummy—which has come to be known as the the Lord of Sipán—were discovered in 1987 in northern Peru. The tomb also held jewels beyond compare and other riches.

The Lord of Sipán rests in an enormous burial complex in the Lambayeque Valley, 17.5 miles (28 kilometers) from the northern Peruvian city of Chiclayo. He was a powerful ruler who lived in the A.D. 200's. The burial site covers almost 74 acres (30 hectares) and includes three grand components: two monumental structures, which were used for religious ceremonies; and a large funerary mound made of adobe, begun in the A.D. 100's and used for 500 years.

This archaeological complex was given the name of Huaca Rajada. A huaca is is an object that represents something revered, typically a monument of some kind. Huaca Rajada was built by the Moche people, a rich culture that arose on the northern coast of Peru 1,000 years before the Inca. The Moche flourished from the A.D. 100's to the 700's. It was a culture of artists, farmers, fishermen, and warriors, that reached a high level of development and had a complex social organization.

The Moche were expert makers of pottery and metalworks. They were also also great architects. They built enormous adobe buildings, truncated pyramids that were accessed via ramps and decorated with yellow and red paint. They carved fantastic *polychromatic* (multicolored) reliefs featuring representations of their gods.

OFFERINGS AND SACRIFICES

The Moche believed in life after death. Persons of superior rank would take with them a wealth of offerings: jewels and ceremonial objects made of gold and silver; objects of copper, turquoise, and *lapis lazuli* (a rare blue stone); *spondylus* shells (rare colorful, spiney shells); as well as pottery, ornaments, and various types of weapons and insignia denoting power. They were also accompanied by other persons on their journeys into the next life.

Buried with the Lord of Sipán were six other people: three young women (possibly wives or concubines who had apparently died some time earlier), two male warriors, and a child. A third male was placed on the roof of the burial chamber as if standing watch. The warriors had amputated feet, as if to prevent them from leaving the tomb.

It is probable that, believing that they would continue serving their lord in another life, they gracefully accepted their deaths in a ritual sacrifice. Along with them, two llamas and a dog were also sacrificed.

This tomb, though the most well-known, is not the only tomb in the large

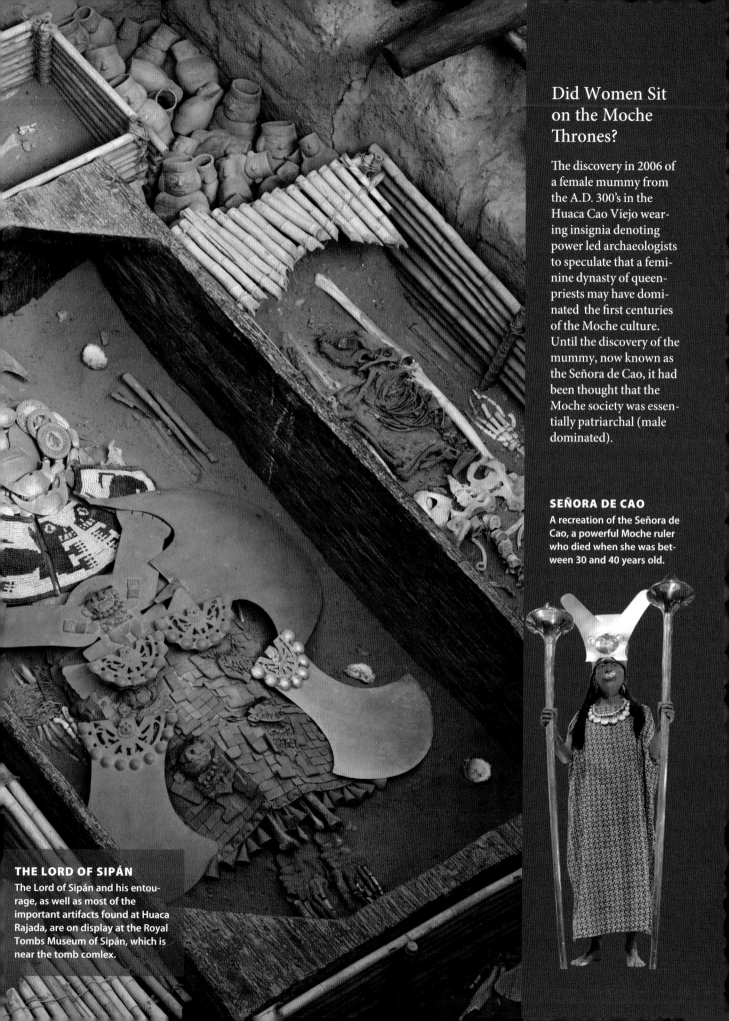

Did Women Sit on the Moche Thrones?

The discovery in 2006 of a female mummy from the A.D. 300's in the Huaca Cao Viejo wearing insignia denoting power led archaeologists to speculate that a feminine dynasty of queen-priests may have dominated the first centuries of the Moche culture. Until the discovery of the mummy, now known as the Señora de Cao, it had been thought that the Moche society was essentially patriarchal (male dominated).

SEÑORA DE CAO

A recreation of the Señora de Cao, a powerful Moche ruler who died when she was between 30 and 40 years old.

THE LORD OF SIPÁN

The Lord of Sipán and his entourage, as well as most of the important artifacts found at Huaca Rajada, are on display at the Royal Tombs Museum of Sipán, which is near the tomb comlex.

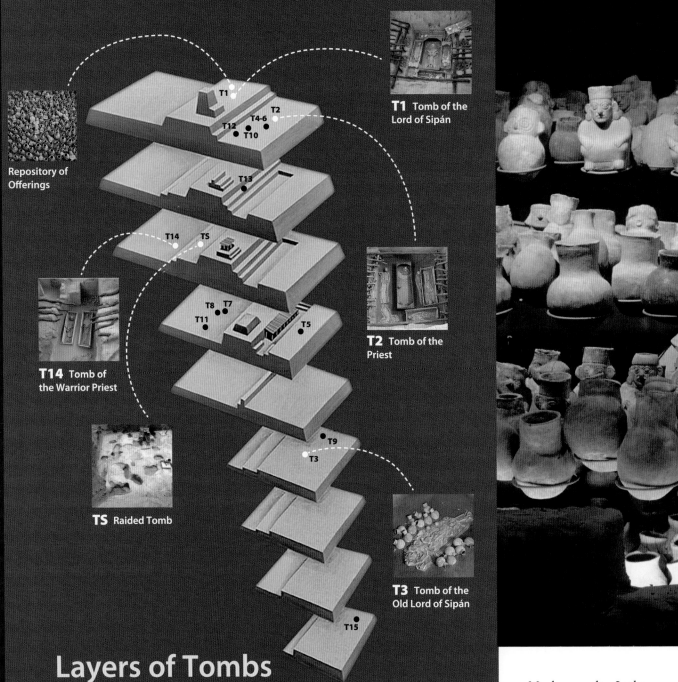

Repository of Offerings

T1 Tomb of the Lord of Sipán

T2 Tomb of the Priest

T14 Tomb of the Warrior Priest

TS Raided Tomb

T3 Tomb of the Old Lord of Sipán

Layers of Tombs

Huaca Rajada is an ancient site that was both ceremonial and sacred. The Moche burial site originally consisted of a stepped pyramid of adobe, but many centuries after its construction, it has been excavated by so many grave robbers that it is now divided into two mounds united by the remains of its central section. This gives rise to its name: Huaca Rajada, the Torn Grave. The region's occasional torrential rains have also contributed to its deterioration. Traditionally, the upper platform was reserved for ceremonial functions. The lower sections housed the mausoleum, where high-level dignitaries of Moche society were buried. However, Huaca Rajada corresponds to an era during which ceremonial and funerary functions were juxtaposed in these sacred sites. As the pyramid was restructured for reasons of maintenance or prestige, new levels were added and new platforms were built on top. Eight architectural construction phases have been detected. The tomb of the Lord of Sipán is found on the top level, while that of the "Old Lord of Sipán" is in one of the lowest levels.

Moche complex. In the burial mound of Sipán, which means "House of the Moon" or "House of the Rulers," up to eight different construction phases corresponding to different eras and hierarchies have been identified.

Between 1987 and 2000, 6 construction phases were discovered, in which as many as 13 different burial sites were excavated. Between 2007 and 2009, 2 more phases were found, with 2 new Moche tombs

Repository of Offerings

Before discovering the Lord of Sipán's tomb, archaeologists found a repository of offerings—a chamber filled with 1,137 ceramic pieces, as well as copper crowns, a mask, shells, and many llama bones. The majority of the ceramic pieces have *anthropomorphous* (of human form) features. The Moche culture is known for its ceramics, which until the discovery of the tombs had been archaeologists' and anthropologists' primary source of information about this culture. Their sculptural finesse combined utility and art. Using clay, they realistically reproduced natural scenes, animals, divinities, economic activities, portraits, etc., documenting their world for the future study. Ceramic materials were also placed in the tomb of the Moche ruler, displayed in an orderly fashion and with ritual finality.

and up to 50 tombs corresponding to later cultures. Among those of the Moche culture, each has a different burial format. The tomb of "the Priest," a contemporary of the Lord of Sipán, suggested his importance: The body wore a headdress of owl feathers and held a copper cup in his hand; and he was flanked by the bodies of two young women, a guardian missing his feet, another young man, a child, a dog, a snake, and a headless llama.

Also notable is the tomb of the "Old Lord of Sipán." His tomb dates from 100 years earlier than the tomb of the young Lord (3 or 4 generations at that time). The Old Lord was accompanied by only two "companions"—a woman and a llama. However, the offerings accompanying him were more complex and varied than those accompanying the young Lord. Archaeologists speculate that he may have fulfilled both political and religious functions.

TREASURE AND LOOTERS
Huaca Rajada, where a museum opened in 2009 to display many of the marvels found there, continues to be excavated, safe from the grave robbers who, in the 1980's, almost managed to make off with its riches.

When archaeologists led by Walter Alva began to work at the site, looters had already stripped several tombs. It is not known whether any of them struck it rich by robbing the tombs of the old lords of Sipán. It

is known that more than one of the looters became ill. Their ailments may have been from breathing cinnabar dust, a substance that releases toxic gases upon contact with air. The Moche dusted cinnabar in tombs before sealing them for the purpose of discouraging tomb raiders. In this way, the priests attempted to ensure that no one disturbed the journey to the "other side" of those who, from their new lives, would continue looking out for their people.

PERU'S VALLEY OF MOCHE
Aerial view of the eroded adobe
pyramids of Sipán, in which archeolo-
gists in 1987 discovered royal tombs
containing mummies and a horde of
gold artifacts. The Moche civilization
flourished in northern Peru from
about A.D. 100 to 800.

The Royal Treasures of Sipán

The Museum of the Royal Tombs of Sipán in Peru contains many objects found among the funerary offerings surrounding the high-level Moche dignitaries buried in Huaca Rajada. The tombs housed a great diversity of offerings, the most exquisite being those of the Lord of Sipán and the Old Lord of Sipán.

The Tumbaga Method

The Moche were extraordinarily talented goldsmiths, displaying great mastery in the smelting of precious metals. They not only smelted copper, gold, and silver but also laminated, shaped, embossed, and soldered them. In their metalwork, they developed complex techniques to give the appearance of gold to objects that were in reality copper, impressing experts to this day. To do this, they used a method called "tumbaga," which was widely used among pre-Columbian societies in Central and South America. This technique consists of a process of depletion gilding, generally with an alloy of 90 percent copper and 10 percent gold. The metal mixture was submerged in ammonia baths to oxidize the copper.

The alloy was then hammered to bring the gold to the surface, while the copper remained in the interior of the sheet.

NECKLACE BEADS
Beads in the shape of an old man's head (left and below). While these particular beads of gold belong to the funerary offerings of the Old Lord of Sipán, necklaces with similarly shaped beads made of gold and silver often formed part of the funerary offerings for Moche aristocrats.

NARIGUERA
Spectacular ceremonial nose ring (left) of the Old Lord of Sipán. Made of gold and silver, it consists of a dignitary with weapons wearing a headdress featuring a bat.

CRAB GOD BREASTPLATE
Ornament in the shape of a crab (above), from the tomb of the Old Lord of Sipán. As a society of fishermen, the Moche modeled their gods after marine life.

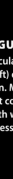

CEREMONIAL DIADEM
Unique diadem with a double representation (right) simultaneously showing the back and palm of the hand. The central figure, the god of Ulluchu, repeats the gesture.

DEITY OF THE ULLUCHU
Gilded copper adornment representing the god of Ulluchu (right). Ulluchu are seeds with anticoagulant properties appearing in blood offerings to Aia Paec, "the Decapitator," the supreme god of the Moche pantheon

Royal Scepter

The scepter of the Lord of Sipán (left) was a symbol of his supreme power. The reliefs carved on the inverted pyramid represent the lord with his warrior garb and combat mace imposing his will on the enemy, a common image on found scepters. Elements of military equipment—including combat maces and slingshots—are represented on the scepter's handle. The silver blade on the end was used in the ritual sacrifice of prisoners.

BREASTPLATE

Radial breastplate (below) made of different colored shells in the form of solar rays.

FELINE HEAD

Feline representation of the supreme god with jaws set with shell encrustations (right).

COXALERA

Gold adornment that hung from the waist with a fold at the top that held a rattle (below). It is made in the shape of the ceremonial knife of the supreme god Aia Paec.

GOLD PEANUTS

Peanut shells (above) that formed part of a necklace for the Lord of Sipán. The necklace consists of 10 gold shells and 10 silver.

BUCKLE AND RATTLE

Gold embossed openwork buckle with the image of the god Aia Paec (above). The orbs contain copper grains that, when shaken, rattle. The buckle was fastened to a belt.

GOLD MASK

Stylized gold mask (above) with the face of a Moche man, discovered in the tomb of the Lord of Sipán.

FELINE DIVINITY

Unique anthropomorphic figure of Aia Paec (left), represented as a feline divinity with an owl-headed serpent headdress. Found in the funerary offerings of the Old Lord of Sipán. The figure formed part of a headdress.

BREASTPLATE AND MASK

Octopus breastplate (left) based on ritual representations of Aia Paec—the principal Moche divinity. It and the attached funerary mask were found in the tomb of the Old Lord of Sipán

Places to See and Visit

OTHER PLACES OF INTEREST

MUSEUM OF THE ROYAL TOMBS OF SIPÁN
SIPÁN, PERU

The Royal Moche Room, in which the Lord of Sipán tomb is exhibited, is the main attraction in this collection. In addition to mummies, the museum has an extraordinary collection of gold artifacts, clothing, jewels, and the various objects making up the funerary offerings of the Moche culture.

SOUTH TYROL MUSEUM OF ARCHAEOLOGY
BOLZANO, ITALY

The Ötzi mummy, "the Iceman," is displayed in a chamber emulating the glacial conditions that kept him exceptionally well-preserved for more than 3,000 years. In addition to the original items found with Ötzi (tools and clothes), the museum has replicas that illustrate life in the Alps during the Bronze Age.

EGYPTIAN MUSEUM
CAIRO, EGYPT

The Egyptian Museum in Cairo contains the world's most extensive collection of pharaonic antiquities. Among its many treasures, the museum contains the mummy of Ramses II and the fabulous contents of Tutankhamun's tomb, including the solid gold mask.

Xi'an, China

WARRIORS

The enormous Museum of Qin Terra-cotta Warriors and Horses is near the city of Xi'an. On display are all of the figures excavated since 1979. After more than three decades of work, around 7,000 figures—ceramics, soldiers, carriages, horses, and weapons—have been unearthed. Almost all have been restored.

HISTORY MUSEUM

Ancient Chinese civilization was born in the province of Shaanxi, and the city of Xi'an was its capital for more than 1,000 years. Thirteen different imperial dynasties were established and reign-ed here. The museum, built in 1983, houses an impressive collection of items that present the country's history through various pieces and exhibits. The exhibit portraying the invention of paper merits special attention.

QIN'S TOMB

The emperor's tomb is a few miles from the museum. It has been calculated that building the entire funerary complex took 38 years. In addition to the terra-cotta army, the complex includes around 400 tombs. The emperor's tomb has not yet been excavated.

Huaqing Hot Springs

These baths, construction of which began in A.D. 720 during the reign of the Tang dynasty, are found near the mausoleum of the emperor Qin Shi Huangdi. The enclave includes several palaces, pools, lookouts, and an enormous artificial lake, as well as sculptures and gardens of great beauty.

SILKEBORG MUSEUM
SILKEBORG, DENMARK

The museum contains the Tollund Man, one of the best known of the "bog bodies." The Elling Woman, another mummy from the area, is also on display; it is presumed that she was sacrificed in some kind of ritual. The museum has created an exhibition on the early Iron Age, in which replicas of clothing from that era, smelting ovens, tools, and other objects are highlighted.

DRENTS MUSEUM
ASSEN, NETHERLANDS

This museum in the Dutch city of Assen houses one of the most important collections of "bog bodies." Within the collection, the Yde Girl, the Weerdinge Men, the Exloërmond Man, and Emmer-Erscheidenveen Man stand out. Other striking pieces in the collection include the oldest canoe in the world, made between 8200 and 7600 B.C., and various metal funerary objects.

Glossary

Anthropomorphous — of human form

Bludgeoned — hit repeatedly with a heavy object

Bronze Age — period when people began to use bronze, an alloy of copper and tin, for tools and weapons, about 3500 B.C.

Chamois — a small goat-like animal that lives in high mountains

Columbarium — place where human ashes are stored

Concubine — a wife of inferior rank to first wife

Cruciform — cross-shaped

Lapis lazuli — a rare blue stone

Mesolithic — middle part of the Stone Age

Mausoleum — a large tomb, especially one above ground

Necropolis —cemetery

Neolithic — late Stone Age

Paleo — ancient

Patriarchal — male-dominated

Polychromatic — multicolored

Pre-Columbian — before 1492

Sarcophagus — a stone coffin

Spondylus shells — rare, colorful spinney seashells

Unique — one of kind

For Further Information

Books

Deem, James M. *Bodies from the Ice: Melting Glaciers and the Recovery of the Past.* Boston: Houghton Mifflin, 2008. Print.

Griffey, Harriet. *Secrets of the Mummies.* New York: DK Pub., 2013. Print.

Malam, John. *100 Things You Should Know about Mummies.* Broomall, PA: Mason Crest, 2011. Print.

Putnam, James, Geoff Brightling, and Peter Hayman. *Pyramid.* New York: DK Pub., 2011. Print.

Sloan, Christopher. *Mummies: Dried, Tanned, Sealed, Drained, Frozen, Embalmed, Stuffed, Wrapped, and Smoked ... and We're Dead Serious.* Washington, D.C.: National Geographic, 2010. Print.

Websites

"Lindow Man." *The British Museum.* Trustees of the British Museum, n.d. Web. 0-7 Feb. 2014.

"Mummy Maker." *BBC History.* BBC, 2014. Web. 07 Feb. 2014.

"Mysterious Mummies of China." *Nova Online.* PBS, 1998. Web. 07 Feb. 2014.

Theban Mapping Project. Theban Mapping Project, 2013. Web. 07 Feb. 2014.

"Tutankhamun: Beneath the Mask." *Science Museum.* The Science Museum, n.d. Web. 07 Feb. 2014.

Index

A

Afterlife, 6, 23, 34, 37
Aia Paec, 41
Alps, 7, 14, 16, 42
Alva, Walter, 14, 15, 37
Atacama Desert, 10

B

Beauty of Xiaohe, 33
Bergman, Folke, 32
Bog bodies, 7, 14, 18-19, 43
Bronze Age, 32, 42
Burials. See Mummies; Tombs

C

Caesar, Julius, 18, 27
Canopic jars, 23
Carter, Howard, 22, 23
Caucasian mummies in China. See
    Indo-European mummies
Ceramics, 37
Chile, 10-12
China, Ancient: mausoleum and
    terra-cotta army, 7, 14, 15, 24-31,
    43; mummies, 7, 14, 15, 32-33
Chinchorro people, 10-12
Cinnabar, 37
Cremation, 9, 13-14

D

Death, 6
Denmark, 18-19, 32, 43
DNA analysis, 6, 10, 12, 16
Drents Museum, 43

E

Egypt, Ancient: mummies, 7, 9,
    12-13, 22-23; museum, 42;
    pyramids, 20-21
Egyptian Museum, 42
Elling Woman, 43
Embalming. See Mummies
Etruscans, 8-9
Excavations, 10; Moche tombs, 36;
    terra-cotta army, 24-26, 28-29;
    Xiaohe mummies, 32

G

Giza, 20-21
Gold, 22, 40-41, 42
Grauballe Man, 18
Great Pyramid, 20

H

Han dynasty, 26, 27
Herod the Great, 11, 14, 15, 31
Herodium, 11, 14, 15, 31
Herodotus, 13
Horses, in tombs, 26, 30
Huaca Rajada tombs, 14, 15, 34-41
Huacas, 12, 14, 34
Huaqing Hot Springs, 43

I

Ice Maiden, 12
Iceman. See Ötzi the Iceman
Inca, 12, 14
Indo-European mummies, 7, 14, 15,
    32-33
Isotopic analysis, 6
Israel, 10-11, 14, 15

K

Khufu, 20

L

Lindow Man, 18
Looting: Egyptian tombs, 20; Shi
    Huangdi's tomb and, 26; Sipán
    tombs, 14, 15, 36, 37
Lord of Sipán, 7, 14, 15, 34-41;
    museum, 42; "Old Lord," 36, 37,
    40, 41

M

Mair, Victor Henry, 14
Mausoleums, 25; Newgrange, 12-13;
    Shi Huangdi, 7, 15, 24, 26-31, 43;
    Sipán, 14
Moche people, 14, 15, 34-41
Mount Li, 24
Mummies, 7, 9; analysis of, 10;
    bog bodies, 7, 14, 18-19, 43;
    Chinchorro, 10-12; Egyptian,
    7, 9, 12-13, 22-23, 42; Inca, 12;
    Indo-Europeans in China, 7, 14,
    15, 32-33; Lord of Sipán, 34, 42;
    Ötzi the Iceman, 7, 14, 16-17, 42
Museum of Qin Terracotta Warriors
    and Horses, 43
Museum of the Royal Tombs of
    Sipán, 15, 40, 41

N

Natron, 23
Neolithic Period, 7, 13-14
Nerthus, 18
Netzer, Ehud, 14, 15, 31
Newgrange passage tomb, 13-14

O

Ötzi the Iceman, 7, 14, 16-17, 42

P

Peat bog bodies. See Bog bodies
Peru: Chinchorro people, 10-12; Lord
    of Sipán, 7, 14, 15, 34-41
Pharaohs, 12, 20-23, 42
Pliny the Elder, 18
Pyramids: Egypt, 7, 20-21; Sipán,
    15, 34, 36, 38-39; tomb of Shi
    Huangdi, 26, 30

Q

Qin dynasty, 26, 27
Qin Shi Huangdi. See Shi Huangdi
Quechua language, 14

R

Ramses II, 23, 42
Reinhard, Johan, 12
Religious sacrifice. See Sacrifice,
    Human
Royal Moche Room, 42

S

Sacrifice, Human: bog bodies, 18,
    19, 42; Inca, 12, 14; Moche
    people, 34; Newgrange, 13; Shi
    Huangdi's tomb, 27
Sarcophagi, 14, 15, 30
Señora de Cao, 35
Shaanxi History Museum, 43
Shi Huangdi, 7, 14, 15, 24-31, 43
Shi Ji (Sima Qian), 26
Silkeborg Museum, 43
Sima Qian, 26-27, 30
Simon, Helmut and Erika, 16
Sipán, 7, 14, 15, 34. See also Lord of
    Sipán
Skeletons, 7
Slavery, 27
South Tyrol Museum of
    Archaeology, 42

Stein, Aurel, 14
Stone Age, 7, 13-14

T
Tacitus, 18
Taklimakan desert, 32
Tarim Basin, 7, 14, 15
Tattoos, 16
Terra-cotta army of Xi'an, 7, 14, 15,
    24-31, 43
Tollund Man, 19, 43
Tombs: Egyptian, 20-23; Etruscan,
    8-9; Herodium, 11, 14, 15;
    Huaca Rajada, 14, 15, 34-41;
    Newgrange, 13-14; Shi Huangdi,
    7, 14, 15, 24-31, 43; sites to see
    and visit, 42-43; studying, 10,
    28-29; Xiaohe, 32-33. See also
    Mausoleums; Pyramids
Tools, 16, 17
Treasures: Egyptian tombs, 20, 22,
    23; Shi Huangdi's tomb, 26-29;
    Sipán, 34-37, 40-41
Tumbaga method, 40
Tutankhamun, 20, 22-23, 42

U
Ulluchu, 40, 41

V
Valley of the Kings, 23
Ventarrón temple, 15

W
West Bank, 14
Women, in Moche culture, 35

X
Xi'an, 15, 24, 43. See also Terra-cotta
    army of Xi'an
Xiaohe Little River Tomb complex,
    32-33
Xu Weihong, 15

Acknowledgments

Pictures:

© ACL
© Age Fotostock
© Alamy Images
© Album
AP Photo
© Corbis Images
© Cordon Press
© Field Museum of Natural History
© Getty Images
© Superstock
© Werner Forman Archive/Egyptian Museum, Cairo